Algernon Charles Swinburne

A Song of Italy

Algernon Charles Swinburne

A Song of Italy

ISBN/EAN: 9783337241889

Printed in Europe, USA, Canada, Australia, Japan

Cover: Foto ©Thomas Meinert / pixelio.de

More available books at **www.hansebooks.com**

ATALANTA.

By ALGERNON C. SWINBURNE.

Fcap. 8vo, cloth, 6s.

JOHN CAMDEN HOTTEN.

OPINIONS OF THE PRESS.

"HE has produced a dramatic poem which abounds from the first page to the last in the finest constituents of poetry—in imagination, fancy, feeling, sentiment, passion, and knowledge of the human heart and soul, combined with a dominant mastery over every species of verse, from the stateliest pomp of epic metre to the fluent sweetness of song. . . . He has something of that creative force which all great poets have had, whether they were Greek, Italian, or English—a native and inborn strength, which scholarship may mould, but can never originate. If, as we are given to understand, Mr. Swinburne is a young writer, we do not hesitate to assert that his volume is extraordinary, not simply for strength and vividness of imagination, but (what is far more remarkable with inexperience) for maturity of power, for completeness of self-control, for absolute mastery over the turbulent forces of adolescent genius. . . . That strange, sad, hopeless mood in which the ancient Greek regarded the mysteries of life and death—that austere setting of the soul against the iron will of destiny which is so full of an immense dignity and pathos—that divinely sorrowful despair of things which can suffer to the miserable end, and sees no after compensation, and yet goes down to death in majesty, and beauty, and power—these characteristics of the old Greek faith, or want of faith, or whatsoever we may call it, are reflected by Mr. Swinburne with amazing truth and discrimination. There are passages in his poem which seem to wring from the very roots of human experience the sharpest extract of our griefs."—LONDON REVIEW, *8th April, 1865.*

" Mr. Swinburne has judged well in his choice of a subject. The legend of Calydon is one of the most beautiful in the whole compass of the Greek mythology; fresh, simple, romantic, solemn, and pathetic, yet without any of those horrors which shock us in the stories of Thebes or Argos—no Jocasta, no Thyestes, but figures full of heroic truth and nobleness, standing out in the clear bright light of the early morning of Greece. . . . A careful study of the Attic dramatists has enabled him to catch their manner, and to reproduce felicitously many of their turns of expression. The scholar is struck, every few lines, by some phrase which he can fancy a direct translation from the Greek, while yet it is in its place both forcible and unaffected. The matter, although not really Greek in its essence, is thrown with great cleverness into a mould which almost beguiles us into forgetting the author, and imagining that we are listening to one of the contemporaries of Euripides who sought to copy the manner of Æschylus. . . . He is, indeed, never more happy than in painting nature, knowing and loving her well, and inspired by her beauty into a vivid force and fulness of expression."—SATURDAY REVIEW, *6th May*, 1865.

"The passion of Althæa is much the finest part of the play. The naturalism of maternal instinct struggling with the feeling of what is due to the shade of her mother and her brothers, goes far beyond the struggle in Antigone or Orestes. Out of many noble passages depicting this feeling we choose the last and most passionate—passionate beyond the limits of Greek passion, and too little ingrained with the Greek awe,—but still exceedingly fine."—SPECTATOR, *April 15th*, 1865.

"He is gifted with no small portion of the all-important divine fire, without which no man can hope to achieve poetic success; he possesses considerable powers of description, a keen eye for natural scenery, and a copious vocabulary of rich yet simple English. . . . We must now part from our author with cordial congratulations on the success with which he has achieved so difficult a task."—TIMES, *June 6th*, 1865.

"'Atalanta in Calydon' is the work of a poet. . . . Let our readers say whether they often meet with pictures lovelier in themselves or more truly Greek than those in the following invocation to Artemis. . . . Many strains equal to the above in force, beauty and rhythmical flow might be cited from the chorus. Those which set forth the brevity of man's life, and the darkness which enfolds it, though almost irreverent in their impeachment of the gods, are singularly fine in expression. . . . We yet know not to what poet since Keats we could turn for a representation at once so large in its design and so graphic in its particulars. In the noble hyperbole of description which raises the boar into the veritable scourge of Artemis, there is imagination of the highest kind. . . . A subject for many a painter to come—a grand word-picture, in which the influence of no contemporary can be traced. . . . In the fervour and beauty of his best passages we find no reflection of any modern writer. . . . We must not close without a reference to the Greek lines, plaintive and full of classic grace, which the writer has prefixed to his work in honour of Walter Savage Landor."—ATHENÆUM, *April 1st*, 1865.

"The choruses are so good, that it is difficult to praise them enough. Were our space unlimited, we would transfer them without abridgment to our columns; as it is not, we can only give a few extracts; but we may fairly assume that every one who cares for poetry of a truly high order will make himself familiar with Mr. Swinburne's drama. . . . As we listen to them they seem to set themselves to a strange but grand music, which lingers long on the ear. . . . . Sometimes we are reminded of Shelley in the lyric passages, but it is more the movement of the verse and its wonderful music, than anything else which suggests a resemblance. . . . Mr. Swinburne has lived with the great Athenian dramatists till his tone of thought has somewhat assimilated to theirs, but he has learnt rather to sympathize with them as a contemporary artist, than to copy them as a modern student."—READER, *April 22nd,* 1865.

" Our extracts have shown that we much prefer to let Mr. Swinburne present his own marvellous earnestness and rich delivery of manner than to essay in this, our necessarily brief review, a lengthened criticism or analysis of such a remarkable work of promise. Apart from the serious endeavour and high devoir to which he has devoted himself in his first appeal to public attention, we would remark the sensuousness, brilliancy, and fervour of the lyrics, which here and there relieve the more sombre and sterner phases of the poem. . . . Assuredly this is the choicest and most complete effort which has for a long time announced that a scholar and a poet has come amongst us."—MORNING HERALD, *April 27th,* 1865.

"One grave error, which Mr. Swinburne has almost entirely avoided, is the use of thoughts or expressions which, current now, would be out of place in a tragedy of Greece. He has, with rare artistic feeling, let scarcely a trace appear of modern life. The Poem is all alive with the life of a classic past . . . . The whole play is instinct with power of varied kinds."—EXAMINER, *July 15th,* 1865.

" We have before said Mr. Swinburne is a subtle analyst of human motive, and possesses great tragic power. The present work shows him to have imagination of the highest order, wonderful play of fancy, and a complete command over every form of versification. . . . He has command of imagery as great as his control of language. He has power which rises to sublimity; passion which deepens into terror ; daring which soars beyond reach or control • . . . We have said enough to convince our readers that we regard this poem as a worthy companion to 'Chastelard,' and look upon its author as permanently enrolled among great English poets."—SUNDAY TIMES, *December 31st,* 1865.

" These lines are marked by that melancholy that always characterizes the poetry in proportion to the absence of faith. . . . Could he have faith, of which there is not a trace throughout the poem, except the miserable vacuum created by its absence, he might do wonders as a poet."—THE TABLET, *August 12th,* 1865.

" As to the tragedy itself, we find in it everything to praise and nothing to censure. It is one of the few really great poems that have been contributed to English literature since the death of Shelley; and it entitles its author at once to a place among the great poets of his country. . . . A tragedy on the Grecian model, which is remarkable for its intense emotional vitality, the richness and reality of its imaginative images, the perfect precision and finish of its construction, and the combined stateliness, severity, and music of its diction."—ALBION, *November 11th,* 1865.

" Not the least remarkable and interesting pages of this volume are those to

which the author has consigned a tribute of veneration to the memory of
Walter Savage Landor, in two compositions of Greek elegiac verse. The first
is a dedication addressed to Landor while living, in the form of a valediction,
on the occasion of his last return to Italy; the second, much the longer of
the two, an elegy on his death. No one who has felt how the spirit of the
Æschylean tragedy breathes through the English poem, will have been sur-
prised to find—rather, every such reader would have been disappointed if he
had not found—that Mr. Swinburne's thoughts move with scarcely less ease
and freedom on a modern theme (if indeed Landor may be properly said to
belong to his own age so much as to that of Pericles and Augustus) in the
language and measures of Callinus and Mimmerus than in his native speech.
Of the Greek we will only say that it is not that of a Cambridge prize ode,
but something much better—even if more open to minute criticism—than the
best of such; not in the least like a cento of dainty classical phrases, but the
fresh original gushing of a true poetical vein, nourished by a mastery of the
foreign language, like that which Landor himself in his Latin poems . . . .
It is evidently the produce, not of the tender lyrical faculty which so often
waits on sensitive youth and afterwards fades into the light of common day,
nor even of the classical culture of which it is itself a signal illustration, but
of an affluent and apprehensive genius, which, with ordinary care and fair
fortune, will take a foremost place in English literature. . . . His abstinence
from all overdrawn conceits is remarkable in a young poet of any time, and his
careful avoidance of the shadowy border land of metaphysics and poetry in
which so many versifiers of our own day take refuge from the open scrutiny
of critical sunlight, deserve full praise and recognition."—EDINBURGH REVIEW,
July, 1865.

CHASTELARD.

By ALGERNON C. SWINBURNE.

Fcap. 8vo, cloth, 7s.

JOHN CAMDEN HOTTEN.

OPINIONS OF THE PRESS.

"THE portraits of Mary and of Chastelard are exaggerated, but only as Michael
Angelo's heroic statues are. The consistent steady madness of Chastelard's
passion, which, mad as it is, lies deeper than madness, and, wild as it
is, burns always without flame, is displayed in a way which is most masterly.

As for the Queen, we are quite of opinion that Mr. Swinburne has brought that woman to light again. It will not do, perhaps, to peer closely into her portrait as it lies in these pages; if we do, we become uneasily conscious of blotchy workmanship, with lights too sudden, and shades too deep, and broken harmonies of colour. But close the book, and look at the portrait reflected from it into the mind, and none was ever painted of her so true. It is a portrait which painters and historians alike have only confused; it awaited a poet's hand to this day, and now we have got it. So think we, at any rate, and in saying so we do not exhaust the praise which is due to the author of 'Chastelard.' The dramatic force of the scenes in the latter half of the poem remains to be applauded, but that, luckily for a critic who has come to the end of his tether, is a thing which can only be applauded and cannot be described; we give it our homage. But it is very much to the purpose of this article, that just when the poem becomes more dramatic its faults begin to disappear; and before we come to the admirable scene between Mary and Chastelard in prison, we are blinded to whatever remains. The fact seems to be that Mr. Swinburne is less a poet than a dramatist; it is certain that he is capable of writing in a way which entitles him to small consideration as the one, and to great consideration as the other. . . . But in any case it can never be denied that he is a true man of genius."—PALL MALL GAZETTE, *April 27th*, 1866.

"The two principal figures stand out boldly, and on them the poet has bestowed all the riches of his genius. . . . . The scene in which, having sent for Chastelard, she talks to him in a strange wild mood between love and regretfulness, is extremely subtle and fine. . . . . It will not be doubted by any one who has the pulse of poetry in his blood that this is noble writing—writing instinct with the highest spirit of the Elizabethan Muse. And in the speech of Chastelard, when waiting for the Queen in her chamber, we have something of the large, imperial style of Shakspeare himself. . . . . The scene between Chastelard and the Queen in prison is also pervaded with the highest inspirations of impassioned poetry; and though the love-ravings of Chastelard almost pass the bounds commonly permitted to poets, the shadow of fate, lying dark and heavy over all, seems to cool and moderate the glow. In passages such as these, Mr. Swinburne again proves his right to take a permanent stand among our English poets. . . . . Of power, he has abundance; of passion, perhaps more than enough; of poetry, in its fierce, luminous, and fiery shapes, a wonderful and prodigal richness. . . . . Whatever his faults, however, he is a man of genius of the most unmistakable mark. We do not know when it has fallen to the lot of any poet to produce within one year two such plays as 'Atalanta in Calydon' and 'Chastelard'—dramas conceived and written in two totally distinct styles, and with marked success in both. . . . . He has earned a conspicuous name with singular quickness, and we trust that even greater triumphs lie before him in his onward path."—LONDON REVIEW, *December 9th*, 1865.

"The choruses in 'Atalanta' were astonishing for their imaginative insight their richness of imagery, their depth of impassioned thought, the nervous suppleness of their language, and the lyrical flow of their versification; and many of the speeches of the characters were full of poetry and dramatic truth. In ' Chastelard,' again, we have a splendid example of the poetry that lies in vehement and absorbing passion; but there is some reason to fear that Mr. Swinburne is wanting in the higher beauty of moral dignity and sweetness."—LONDON REVIEW, *December 30th*, 1865.

" We can only say that it abounds in passages of great poetic merit, and the passion of love is described with all that delicacy and vivid ness that can only be found in the writings of a poet endowed with extraordinary genius. Mr. Swinburne has well comprehended the character of Mary Stuart, and she is made to stand before the reader a reality, her nature being wonderfully well exhibited. Other characters are represented with marvellous distinctness, and give to the tragedy interest and vitality."—PUBLIC OPINION, *December 16th*, 1865.

" The style is so forcible that there is little that would render the play unfit for the stage, were it not for the great amount of amativeness which the parties have to display before they are disposed of."—COURT CIRCULAR, *December 23rd*, 1865.

" The picture with which this burst concludes, though too much elaborated, has undeniable grandeur. We could point out passages which, in a dramatic point of view, are yet finer. Those given to Mary Beaton—the only touching character in the play—often reach the height of tragic intensity. Nor is it to be disputed that Mr. Swinburne shows at times a keen insight into the subtleties of human motive, but his chief characters are out of the pale of our sympathy; besid s being inherently vicious, the language will offend not only those who have reverence, but those who have taste."—ATHENÆUM, *December 23rd*, 1865.

" A trage ly—in which we think he best develops his genius. Once before we s id we thought his genius essentially lyric, but he himself has convinced us, not of the contrary, but of the co-existence in him of the dramatic and lyric power."—COURT JOURNAL, *December 19th*, 1865.

" The poem, in fact, is morally repulsive, and all its gilding of fancy and feeling only makes the picture more revolting . . . The dramatic power, the grace of the beauty of the tragedy no one can deny. . . . His insight into hidden human motives is marvellously indicated. Altogether, if the poem fails to please, that must be attributed to the subject and the author's mind of it, not to any lack of workmanship of the very highest and most delicate order."—ATLAS, *December 30th*, 1865.

" It is an unpleasant book, and one by all means to be kept out of the hands of the young and pure-minded, for the licentiousness of many of the images and profanity of not a few of the sentiments are such as happily are not often found in English poets. . . . We cannot doubt that the le s sensuous brotherhood of our Northern poets, would join us in denouncing with indignation and disgust such a lamentable prostitution of the English muse."—JOHN BULL, *December 23rd*, 1865.

" There are two parts of the play deserving of special praise—the second act, and the closing scenes of the fifth. It is in these, and more particularly in the latter, that Mr. Swinburne displays a combination of dramatic and poetic power beyond what is seen in anything that his pen has yet produced. . . . Were it not for their exquisite elegance of expression, these constant exhibitions of passion would deserve severe reprobation. . . . Regarding the work as a whole, we must thank Mr. Swinburne for a dramatic poem of great power, careful elaboration of plot, artistic disposition of scenes; for admirable descriptions of human emotion and passion; for terse, forcible, yet swe t expression, and a generally scrupulous melody of rhythm."—READER, *December 2nd,* 1865.

"Mr. Swinburne has written a tragedy, which not only is one of the most remarkable productions of modern days, but which in originality of conception and boldness of treatment has never been surpassed. The triumph which Mr. Swinb rne has achi ved in 'Chastelard' is the more noteworthy, si ce the splendid gifts of which its composition proclaims him the possessor are totally distinct from those which in ' Atalanta in Calydon' gained him a foremost position among modern poets. In the earlier production, amid all the sublime imagery and lyrical sweetness, the grace truly classic, the boldness of thought and the exquisite charm of versification which constituted it a work of accomplished and all but unrivalled beauty, there was no foreshadowing of the dramatic fire and the weird and almost unholy power which characterize its successor. . . . From this point, where the interest has already reached what appears a climax, each situation is more dramatic and more stirring than the one preceding it. The skill with which—the passions being already at white heat—the action is heightened without anti-climax is absolutely wonderful. . . . The last few words we give in their integrity; no word of ours can add aught to their terrible pathos and dramatic force. With them, and without an added word, we shall conclude our notice of this most remarkable trage y of modern times."—SUNDAY TIMES, *December 3rd,* 1865.

"Here, in his new poem of ' Chastelard,' is Mr. Algernon Swinburne writing French chansons of which Chastelard himself or Ronsard might have been proud. So good are they that by many they are imagined to be merely quotations, transcripts from the original French author. But there is no doubt they are Mr. Swinburne's own composition. Here are two which are exquisite in taste, feeling, and spirit."—MORNING STA , *December 25th,* 1865.

"Here and there occur passages which we unhesitatingly affirm are not surpassed in the language."—LIVERPOOL ALBION, *January 6th,* 1866.

"The public to which Mr. Swinburne appeals will consist exclusively of those readers who enjoy a work of art for its own sake, and who care more for the power of the representation than for any worth in what is represented. . . . Mr. Swinburne has produced a poem which many may dislike but which none can contemn, which many will lay down unread but which few will read once only. It cannot be called an advance upon ' Atalanta,' for it is something totally different, except in its disregard of conventional proprieties, and its independence of the poetical habits of the day. There is the same richness without tawdriness of language, the same novelty without strangeness of expression, the same continual sense of the indispensable duty of melody in verse, which some of our most pretentious poets either forget or disown. . . . The scene in the Queen's chamber is very beautiful, but ingeniously wicked as the rest. . . . For dexterity of fence, both in feeling and language, this scene may rank with the master-pieces of our older drama. . . . The gyrations are so unexpected, and the changes so numerous, that in less masterly hands the effect would be rather that of a psychological puzzle than of a dramatic evolution. . . . It is impossible that this play should not highly raise Mr. Swinburne's reputation. There are artistic defects in it, but not to be mentioned beside the artistic merits. His preface to Moxon's 'Selections from Byron' is another instance of the fact, too often forgotten, that there is no education for the writing of superior prose like the serious practice of poetry; and with this double power, Mr. Swinburne's future career must be an object of much interest to all who estimate aright the worth and weight of British literature in the intellectual and moral history of mankind."—FORTNIGHTLY REVIEW, *April 15th*, 1866.

"He fills out this bold outline, and supplies missing links in the story, and imparts life and form and colour to the whole picture, and reproduces contemporaneous personages and scenery, and, with deep probing of human nature and fine play of imagination, unveils the pathetic tragedy that has so long slept hidden in the dry and trite historic page. The result is a masterpiece of literary art, whether contempl ted as the conception of character, ideals of love and heroism, treatment of a grand and moving theme, majesty, beauty, and purity of style, or lesson to the heart and mind."—THE ALBION, *December 23rd*, 1865.

"The story is vaguely and ineffectively presented. There is little to relieve the repulsive character of the whole tone of the play. It dwells pertinaciously and too warmly upon scenes which are neither noble, edifying, nor decent."—BOSTON DAILY ADVERTISER, *December 14th*, 1865.

"We have but re-echoed the judgment of all competent critics, in saying that Swinburne rightfully ranks with the few great poets of this and of other ages. His present work is one of the finest artistic efforts which we have ever chanced to encounter. It has more human interest than his 'Atalanta in Calydon,' while it is couched in the same vigorous and splendid diction and 'is richly dight' with melodious and sweetly magnificent songs. . . . His portraiture is one of the amplest, most thoroughly elaborated, and most gorgeously coloured, in the whole wide range of British poetry."—NEW YORK WEEKLY REVIEW, *December 9th*, 1865.

"The sustained and elastic strength of the fourth act, in which the turns and windings of Mary's will as Chastelard's death are drawn out—her perplexity, ruthlessness, contempt for a weak man and for a cruel unknightly man, fear of public scorn, remorse for her love, vindictive bitterness against Darnley, all chasing one another over her mind, with the subtlest changes—make one of the most superb scenes for which a drama of character gives room. We feel that the writer is rejoicing in his own skill in unravelling the changeful mysteries of a highly complex character. He exults in his mastery over the Queen's rapid passage from one mood to another, and in the magic by which he can produce and control her Protean transformations."—SATURDAY REVIEW, *May 26th*, 1866.

A SONG OF ITALY.

A

SONG OF ITALY.

BY

ALGERNON CHARLES SWINBURNE.

LONDON:
JOHN CAMDEN HOTTEN, PICCADILLY.
1867.

INSCRIBED,

WITH ALL DEVOTION AND REVERENCE,

TO

JOSEPH MAZZINI.

A SONG OF ITALY.

Upon a windy night of stars that fell
   At the wind's spoken spell,
Swept with sharp strokes of agonizing light
   From the clear gulf of night,
Between the fixed and fallen glories one
   Against my vision shone,
More fair and fearful and divine than they
   That measure night and day,
And worthier worship; and within mine
    eyes
   The formless folded skies

Took shape and were unfolded like as flowers.
   And I beheld the hours
As maidens, and the days as labouring men,
   And the soft nights again
As wearied women to their own souls wed,
   And ages as the dead.
And over these living, and them that died,
   From one to the other side
A lordlier light than comes of earth or air
   Made the world's future fair.
A woman like to love in face, but not
   A thing of transient lot—
And like to hope, but having hold on
      truth—
   And like to joy or youth,
Save that upon the rock her feet were set—
   And like what men forget,

Faith, innocence, high thought, laborious
    peace—

    And yet like none of these,

Being not as these are mortal, but with eyes

    That sounded the deep skies

And clove like wings or arrows their clear
    way

    Through night and dawn and day—

So fair a presence over star and sun

    Stood, making these as one.

For in the shadow of her shape were all

    Darkened and held in thrall,

So mightier rose she past them ; and I felt

    Whose form, whose likeness knelt

With covered hair and face and clasped her
    knees ;

    And knew the first of these

Was Freedom, and the second Italy.
  And what sad words said she
For mine own grief I knew not, nor had
    heart
  Therewith to bear my part
And set my songs to sorrow ; nor to hear
  How tear by sacred tear
Fell from her eyes as flowers or notes that
    fall
  In some slain feaster's hall
Where in mid music and melodious breath
  Men singing have seen death.
So fair, so lost, so sweet she knelt ; or so
  In our lost eyes below
Seemed to us sorrowing ; and her speech being
    said,
  Fell, as one who falls dead.

And for a little she too wept, who stood
    Above the dust and blood
And thrones and troubles of the world;
        then spake,
    As who bids dead men wake.

" Because the years were heavy on thy head;
    Because dead things are dead;
Because thy chosen on hill-side, city and
        plain
    Are shed as drops of rain;
Because all earth was black, all heaven was
        blind,
    And we cast out of mind;
Because men wept, saying *Freedom*, knowing
        of thee,
    Child, that thou wast not free;

Because wherever blood was not shame was
  Where thy pure foot did pass;
Because on Promethean rocks distent
  Thee fouler eagles rent;
Because a serpent stains with slime and foam
  This that is not thy Rome;
Child of my womb, whose limbs were made in
    me,
  Have I forgotten thee?
In all thy dreams through all these years on
    wing,
  Hast thou dreamed such a thing?
The mortal mother-bird outsoars her nest,
  The child outgrows the breast;
But suns as stars shall fall from heaven and
    cease,
  Ere we twain be as these;

Yea, utmost skies forget their utmost sun,

    Ere we twain be not one.

My lesser jewels sewn on skirt and hem,

    I have no heed of them

Obscured and flawed by sloth or craft or

    power ;

    But thou, that wast my flower,

The blossom bound between my brows and

    worn

    In sight of even and morn

From the last ember of the flameless west

    To the dawn's baring breast—

I were not Freedom if thou wert not free,

    Nor thou wert Italy.

O mystic rose ingrained with blood, im-

    pearled

    With tears of all the world !

The torpor of their blind brute-ridden
  trance
  Kills England and chills France;
And Spain sobs hard through strangling blood;
  and snows
  Hide the huge eastern woes.
But thou, twin-born with morning, nursed of
  noon,
  And blessed of star and moon!
What shall avail to assail thee any more,
  From sacred shore to shore?
Have Time and Love not knelt down at thy
  feet,
  Thy sore, thy soiled, thy sweet,
Fresh from the flints and mire of murderous
  ways
  And dust of travelling days?

Hath Time not kissed them, Love not washed
them fair,
And wiped with tears and hair?
Though God forget thee, I will not forget;
Though heaven and earth be set
Against thee, O unconquerable child,
Abused, abased, reviled,
Lift thou not less from no funereal bed
Thine undishonoured head;
Love thou not less, by lips of thine once
prest,
This my now barren breast;
Seek thou not less, being well assured
thereof,
O child, my latest love.
For now the barren bosom shall bear fruit,
Songs leap from lips long mute,

And with my milk the mouths of nations fed
  Again be glad and red
That were worn white with hunger and sor-
      row and thirst ;
  And thou, most fair and first,
Thou whose warm hands and sweet live lips I
    feel
  Upon me for a seal,
Thou whose least looks, whose smiles and
    little sighs,
  Whose passionate pure eyes,
Whose dear fair limbs that neither bonds could
    bruise
  Nor hate of men misuse,
Whose flower-like breath and bosom, O my
    child,
  O mine and undefiled,

Fill with such tears as burn like bitter wine

    These mother's eyes of mine,

Thrill with huge passions and primeval

    pains

    The fulness of my veins.

O sweetest head seen higher than any stands,

    I touch thee with mine hands,

I lay my lips upon thee, O thou most sweet,

    To lift thee on thy feet

And with the fire of mine to fill thine eyes;

    I say unto thee, Arise."

She ceased, and heaven was full of flame and

    sound,

    And earth's old limbs unbound

Shone and waxed warm with fiery dew and seed

    Shed through her at this her need:

And highest in heaven, a mother and full of
   grace,
   With no more covered face,
With no more lifted hands and bended knees,
   Rose, as from sacred seas
Love, when old time was full of plenteous
   springs,
   That fairest-born of things,
The land that holds the rest in tender thrall
   For love's sake in them all,
That binds with words and holds with eyes and
   hands
   All hearts in all men's lands.
So died the dream whence rose the live desire
   That here takes form and fire,
A spirit from the splendid grave of sleep
   Risen, that ye should not weep,

Should not weep more nor ever, O ye that hear
   And ever have held her dear,
Seeing now indeed she weeps not who wept
   sore,
   And sleeps not any more.
Hearken ye towards her, O people, exalt your
   eyes ;
   Is this a thing that dies ?

Italia ! by the passion of the pain
   That bent and rent thy chain ;
Italia ! by the breaking of the bands,
   The shaking of the lands ;
Beloved, O men's mother, O men's queen,
   Arise, appear, be seen !
Arise, array thyself in manifold
   Queen's raiment of wrought gold ;

With girdles of green freedom, and with
    red
  Roses, and white snow shed
Above the flush and frondage of the hills
  That all thy deep dawn fills
And all thy clear night veils and warms with
    wings
  Spread till the morning sings;
The rose of resurrection, and the bright
  Breast lavish of the light,
The lady lily like the snowy sky
  Ere the stars wholly die;
As red as blood, and whiter than a wave,
  Flowers grown as from thy grave,
From the green fruitful grass in Maytime
    hot,
  Thy grave, where thou art not.

Gather the grass and weave, in sacred sign
   Of the ancient earth divine,
The holy heart of things, the seed of birth,
   The mystical warm earth.
O thou her flower of flowers, with treble braid
   Be thy sweet head arrayed,
In witness of her mighty motherhood
   Who bore thee and found thee good,
Her fairest-born of children, on whose head
   Her green and white and red
Are hope and light and life, inviolate
   Of any latter fate.
Fly, O our flag, through deep Italian air,
   Above the flags that were,
The dusty shreds of shameful battle-flags
   Trampled and rent in rags,

As withering woods in autumn's bitterest
    breath
    Yellow, and black as death;
Black as crushed worms that sicken in the
    sense,
    And yellow as pestilence.
Fly, green as summer and red as dawn and
    white
    As the live heart of light,
The blind bright womb of colour unborn,
    that brings
    Forth all fair forms of things,
As freedom all fair forms of nations dyed
    In divers-coloured pride.
Fly fleet as wind on every wind that
    blows
    Between her seas and snows,

From Alpine white, from Tuscan green, and
    where
  Vesuvius reddens air.
Fly! and let all men see it, and all kings
    wail,
  And priests wax faint and pale,
And the cold hordes that moan in misty places
  And the funereal races
And the sick serfs of lands that wait and wane
  See thee and hate thee in vain.
In the clear laughter of all winds and waves,
  In the blown grass of graves,
In the long sound of fluctuant boughs of
    trees,
  In the broad breath of seas,
Bid the sound of thy flying folds be heard;
  And as a spoken word

Full of that fair god and that merciless
    Who rends the Pythoness,
So be the sound and so the fire that saith
    She feels her ancient breath
And the old blood move in her immortal
        veins.

    Strange travail and strong pains,
Our mother, hast thou borne these many years,
    While thy pure blood and tears
Mixed with the Tyrrhene and the Adrian
        sea ;
    Light things were said of thee,
As of one buried deep among the dead ;
    Yea, she hath been, they said,
She was when time was younger, and is not ;
    The very cerecloths rot

That flutter in the dusty wind of death,
  Not moving with her breath ;
Far seasons and forgotten years enfold
  Her dead corpse old and cold
With many windy winters and pale springs ;
  She is none of this world's things.
Though her dead head like a live garland wear
  The golden-growing hair
That flows over her breast down to her feet,
  Dead queens, whose life was sweet
In sight of all men living, have been found
  So cold, so clad, so crowned,
With all things faded and with one thing fair,
  Their old immortal hair,
When flesh and bone turned dust at touch of
    day :
  And she is dead as they.

So men said sadly, mocking ; so the slave,
    Whose life was his soul's grave ;
So, pale or red with change of fast and feast,
    The sanguine-sandalled priest ;
So the Austrian, when his fortune came to
    flood,
    And the warm wave was blood ;
With wings that widened and with beak that
    smote,
    So shrieked through either throat
From the hot horror of its northern nest
    That double-headed pest ;
So, triple-crowned with fear and fraud and
    shame,
    He of whom treason came,
The herdsman of the Gadarean swine ;
    So all his ravening kine,

Made fat with poisonous pasture; so not
  we,
  Mother, beholding thee.
Make answer, O the crown of all our slain,
  Ye that were one, being twain,
Twain brethren, twin-born to the second
  birth,
  Chosen out of all our earth
To be the prophesying stars that say
  How hard is night on day,
Stars in serene and sudden heaven re-risen
  Before the sun break prison
And ere the moon be wasted; fair first flowers
  In that red wreath of ours,
Woven with the lives of all whose lives were
  shed
  To crown their mother's head

With leaves of civic cypress and thick
   yew,
  Till the olive bind it too,
Olive and laurel and all loftier leaves
  That victory wears or weaves
At her fair feet for her beloved brow;
  Hear, for she too hears now,
O Pisacane, from Calabrian sands;
  O all heroic hands
Close on the sword-hilt, hands of all her
   dead;
  O many a holy head,
Bowed for her sake even to her reddening
   dust;
  O chosen, O pure and just,
Who counted for a small thing life's estate,
  And died, and made it great;

Ye whose names mix with all her memories ; ye
    Who rather chose to see
Death, than our more intolerable things ;
    Thou whose name withers kings,
Agesilao ; thou too, O chiefliest thou,
    The slayer of splendid brow,
Laid where the lying lips of fear deride
    The foiled tyrannicide,
Foiled, fallen, slain, scorned, and happy ; being
      in fame,
    Felice, like thy name,
Not like thy fortune ; father of the fight,
    Having in hand our light.
Ah, happy ! for that sudden-swerving hand
    Flung light on all thy land,
Yea, lit blind France with compulsory ray,
    Driven down a righteous way ;

Ah, happiest! for from thee the wars began,
　From thee the fresh springs ran;
From thee the lady land that queens the earth
　Gat as she gave new birth.
O sweet mute mouths, O all fair dead of
　　ours,
　Fair in her eyes as flowers,
Fair without feature, vocal without voice,
　Strong without strength, rejoice!
Hear it with ears that hear not, and on eyes
　That see not let it rise,
Rise as a sundawn; be it as dew that drips
　On dumb and dusty lips;
Eyes have ye not, and see it; neither ears,
　And there is none but hears.
This is the same for whom ye bled and wept;
　She was not dead, but slept.

This is that very Italy which was
    And is and shall not pass.

But thou, though all were not well done, O chief,
    Must thou take shame or grief?
Because one man is not as thou or ten,
    Must thou take shame for men ?
Because the supreme sunrise is not yet,
    Is the young dew not wet ?
Wilt thou not yet abide a little while,
    Soul without fear or guile,
Mazzini,—O our prophet, O our priest,
    A little while at least ?
A little hour of doubt and of control,
    Sustain thy sacred soul ;
Withhold thine heart, our father, but an hour ;
    Is it not here, the flower,

Is it not blown and fragrant from the root,

And shall not be the fruit?

Thy children, even thy people thou hast

made,

Thine, with thy words arrayed,

Clothed with thy thoughts and girt with thy

desires,

Yearn up toward thee as fires.

Art thou not father, O father, of all these?

From thine own Genoese

To where of nights the lower extreme lagune

Feels its Venetian moon,

Nor suckling's mouth nor mother's breast set

free,

But hath that grace through thee.

The milk of life on death's unnatural brink

Thou gavest them to drink,

The natural milk of freedom; and again

 They drank, and they were men.

The wine and honey of freedom and of
  faith

 They drank, and cast off death.

Bear with them now; thou art holier: yet
  endure,

 Till they as thou be pure.

Their swords at least that stemmed half
  Austria's tide

 Bade all its bulk divide;

Else, though fate bade them for a breath's
  space fall,

 She had not fallen at all.

Not by their hands they made time's promise
  true;

 Not by their hands, but through.

Nor on Custozza ran their blood to waste,
  Nor fell their fame defaced
Whom stormiest Adria with tumultuous tides
  Whirls undersea and hides.
Not his, who from the sudden-settling deck
  Looked over death and wreck
To where the mother's bosom shone, who
    smiled
  As he, so dying, her child;
For he smiled surely, dying, to mix his death
  With her memorial breath ;
Smiled, being most sure of her, that in no wise,
  Die whoso will, she dies :
And she smiled surely, fair and far above,
  Wept not, but smiled for love.
Thou too, O splendour of the sudden sword
  That drove the crews abhorred

From Naples and the siren-footed strand,

    Flash from thy master's hand,

Shine from the middle summer of the seas

    To the old Æolides,

Outshine their fiery fumes of burning night,

    Sword, with thy midday light ;

Flame as a beacon from the Tyrrhene foam

    To the rent heart of Rome,

From the island of her lover and thy lord,

    Her saviour and her sword.

In the fierce year of failure and of fame,

    Art thou not yet the same

That wert as lightning swifter than all

       wings

    In the blind face of kings ?

When priests took counsel to devise despair,

    And princes to forswear,

She clasped thee, O her sword and flag-
    bearer
  And staff and shield to her,
O Garibaldi ; need was hers and grief,
  Of thee and of the chief,
And of another girt in arms to stand
  As good of hope and hand,
As high of soul and happy, albeit indeed
  The heart should burn and bleed,
So but the spirit shake not nor the breast
  Swerve, but abide its rest.
As theirs did and as thine, though ruin
    clomb
  The highest wall of Rome,
Though treason stained and spilt her lustral
    water,
  And slaves led slaves to slaughter,

And priests, praying and slaying, watched them
  pass
  From a strange France, alas,
That was not freedom ; yet when these were
  past,
  Thy sword and thou stood fast,
Till new men seeing thee where Sicilian waves
  Hear now no sound of slaves,
And where thy sacred blood is fragrant still
  Upon the Bitter Hill,
Seeing by that blood one country saved and
  stained,
  Less loved thee crowned than chained,
And less now only than the chief : for he,
  Father of Italy,
Upbore in holy hands the babe new-born
  Through loss and sorrow and scorn,

Of no man led, of many men reviled;
    Till lo, the new-born child
Gone from between his hands, and in its place,
    Lo, the fair mother's face.
Blessed is he of all men, being in one
    As father to her and son,
Blessed of all men living, that he found
    Her weak limbs bared and bound,
And in his arms and in his bosom bore,
    And as a garment wore
Her weight of want, and as a royal dress
    Put on her weariness.
As in faith's hoariest histories men read,
    The strong man bore at need
Through roaring rapids when all heaven was
      wild
    The likeness of a child

That still waxed greater and heavier as he
    trod,
    And altered, and was God.
Praise him, O winds that move the molten
    air,
    O light of days that were,
And light of days that shall be ; land and sea,
    And heaven and Italy :
Praise him, O storm and summer, shore and
    wave,
    O skies and every grave ;
O weeping hopes, O memories beyond tears,
    O many and murmuring years,
O sounds far off in time and visions far,
    O sorrow with thy star,
And joy with all thy beacons ; ye that mourn,
    And ye whose light is born ;

O fallen faces, and O souls arisen,
  Praise him from tomb and prison,
Praise him from heaven and sunlight ; and ye
    floods,
  And windy waves of woods ;
Ye valleys and wild vineyards, ye lit lakes
  And happier hillside brakes,
Untrampled by the accursed feet that trod
  Fields golden from their god,
Fields of their god forsaken, whereof none
  Sees his face in the sun,
Hears his voice from the floweriest wilder-
    nesses ;
  And, barren of his tresses,
Ye bays unplucked and laurels unentwined,
  That no men break or bind,
And myrtles long forgetful of the sword,
  And olives unadored,

Wisdom and love, white hands that save and
    slay,
    Praise him ; and ye as they,
Praise him, O gracious might of dews and rains
    That feed the purple plains,
O sacred sunbeams bright as bare steel drawn,
    O cloud and fire and dawn ;
Red hills of flame, white Alps, green Apen-
    nines,
    Banners of blowing pines,
Standards of stormy snows, flags of light leaves,
    Three wherewith Freedom weaves
One ensign that once woven and once unfurled
    Makes day of all a world,
Makes blind their eyes who knew not, and
    outbraves
    The waste of iron waves ;

Ye fields of yellow fulness, ye fresh fountains,

    And mists of many mountains ;

Ye moons and seasons, and ye days and nights ;

    Ye starry-headed heights,

And gorges melting sunward from the snow,

    And all strong streams that flow

Tender as tears, and fair as faith, and pure

    As hearts made sad and sure

At once by many sufferings and one love ;

    O mystic deathless dove

Held to the heart of earth and in her hands

    Cherished, O lily of lands,

White rose of time, dear dream of praises

        past—

    For such as these thou wast,

That art as eagles setting to the sun,

    As fawns that leap and run,

As a sword carven with keen floral gold,
   Sword for an armed god's hold,
Flower for a crowned god's forehead—O our
      land,
   Reach forth thine holiest hand,
O mother of many sons and memories,
   Stretch out thine hand to his
That raised and gave thee life to run and
      leap
   When thou wast full of sleep,
That touched and stung thee with young blood
      and breath
   When thou wast hard on death.
Praise him, O all her cities and her crowns,
   Her towers and thrones of towns;
O noblest Brescia, scarred from foot to head
   And breast-deep in the dead,

Praise him from all the glories of thy graves

    That yellow Mela laves

With gentle and golden water, whose fair flood

    Ran wider with thy blood ;

Praise him, O born of that heroic breast,

    O nursed thereat and blest,

Verona, fairer than thy mother fair,

    But not more brave to bear ;

Praise him, O Milan, whose imperial tread

    Bruised once the German head ;

Whose might, by northern swords left desolate,

    Set foot on fear and fate ;

Praise him, O long mute mouth of melodies,

    Mantua, with louder keys,

With mightier chords of music even than

    rolled

    From the large harps of old,

When thy sweet singer of golden throat and
    tongue
  Praising his tyrant sung ;
Though now thou sing not as of other days,
  Learn late a better praise.
Not with the sick sweet lips of slaves that sing,
  Praise thou no priest or king,
No brow-bound laurel of discoloured leaf,
  But him, the crownless chief.
Praise him, O star of sun-forgotten times,
  Among their creeds and crimes
That wast a fire of witness in the night,
  Padua, the wise men's light ;
Praise him, O sacred Venice, and the sea
  That now exults through thee,
Full of the mighty morning and the sun,
  Free of things dead and done ;

Praise him from all the years of thy great
    grief,
    That shook thee like a leaf
With winds and snows of torment, rain that
    fell
    Red as the rains of hell,
Storms of black thunder and of yellow flame,
    And all ill things but shame ;
Praise him with all thy holy heart and strength ;
    Through thy walls' breadth and length
Praise him with all thy people, that their
    voice
    Bid the strong soul rejoice,
The fair clear supreme spirit beyond stain,
    Pure as the depth of pain,
High as the head of suffering, and secure
    As all things that endure.

More than thy blind lord of an hundred
    years,
    Whose name our memory hears,
Home-bound from harbours of the Byzantine
    Made tributary of thine,
Praise him who gave no gifts from oversea,
    But gave thyself to thee.
O mother Genoa, through all years that run,
    More than that other son,
Who first beyond the seals of sunset prest
    Even to the unfooted west,
Whose back-blown flag scared from their
    sheltering seas
    The unknown Atlantides,
And as flame climbs through cloud and vapour
    clomb
    Through streams of storm and foam,

Till half in sight they saw land heave and
    swim—
More than this man praise him.
One found a world new-born from virgin sea ;
    And one found Italy.
O heavenliest Florence, from the mouths of
    flowers
Fed by melodious hours,
From each sweet mouth that kisses light and
    air,
Thou whom thy fate made fair,
As a bound vine or any flowering tree,
    Praise him who made thee free.
For no grape-gatherers trampling out the wine
    Tread thee, the fairest vine ;
For no man binds thee, no man bruises, none
    Does with thee as these have done.

From where spring hears loud through her
    long-lit vales
      Triumphant nightingales,
In many a fold of fiery foliage hidden,
      Withheld as things forbidden,
But clamorous with innumerable delight
      In May's red, green, and white,
In the far-floated standard of the spring,
      That bids men also sing,
Our flower of flags, our witness that we are
    free,
      Our lamp for land and sea ;
From where Majano feels through corn and
    vine
      Spring move and melt as wine,
And Fiesole's embracing arms enclose
      The immeasurable rose ;

From hill-sides plumed with pine, and heights
　　wind-worn
　　That feel the refluent morn,
Or where the moon's face warm and passionate
　　Burns, and men's hearts grow great,
And the swoln eyelids labour with sweet
　　tears,
　　And in their burning ears
Sound throbs like flame, and in their eyes new
　　light,
　　Kindles the trembling night ;
From faint illumined fields and starry valleys
　　Wherefrom the hill-wind sallies,
From Vallombrosa, from Valdarno raise
　　One Tuscan tune of praise.
O lordly city of the field of death,
　　Praise him with equal breath,

From sleeping streets and gardens, and the
stream
That threads them as a dream
Threads without light the untravelled ways of
sleep
With eyes that smile or weep ;
From the sweet sombre beauty of wave and
wall
That fades and does not fall ;
From coloured domes and cloisters fair with
fame,
Praise thou and thine his name.
Thou too, O little laurelled town of towers,
Clothed with the flame of flowers,
From windy ramparts girdled with young
gold,
From thy sweet hill-side fold

Of wallflowers and the acacia's belted bloom

    And every blowing plume,

Halls that saw Dante speaking, chapels fair

    As the outer hills and air,

Praise him who feeds the fire that Dante

    fed,

    Our highest heroic head,

Whose eyes behold through floated cloud and

    flame

    The maiden face of fame

Like April in Valdelsa ; fair as flowers,

    And patient as the hours ;

Sad with slow sense of time, and bright with

    faith

    That levels life and death ;

The final fame, that with a foot sublime

    Treads down reluctant time ;

The fame that waits and watches and is wise,

   A virgin with chaste eyes,

A goddess who takes hands with great men's

     grief;

   Praise her, and him, our chief.

Praise him, O Siena, and thou her deep green

     spring,

   O Fonte Branda, sing :

Shout from the red clefts of thy fiery crags,

   Shake out thy flying flags

In the long wind that streams from hill to hill ;

   Bid thy full music fill

The desolate red waste of sunset air

   And fields the old time saw fair,

But now the hours ring void through ruined

     lands,

   Wild work of mortal hands ;

Yet through thy dead Maremma let his name
  Take flight and pass in flame,
And the red ruin of disastrous hours
  Shall quicken into flowers.
Praise him, O fiery child of sun and sea,
  Naples, who bade thee be ;
For till he sent the swords that scourge and
    save,
  Thou wast not, but thy grave.
But more than all these praise him and give
    thanks,
  Thou, from thy Tiber's banks,
From all thine hills and from thy supreme
    dome,
  Praise him, O risen Rome.
Let all thy children cities at thy knee
  Lift up their voice with thee,   .

Saying " for thy love's sake and our perished
    grief
  We laud thee, O our chief ;"
Saying " for thine hand and help when hope
    was dead
  We thank thee, O our head ;"
Saying " for thy voice and face within our
    sight
  We bless thee, O our light ;
For waters cleansing us from days defiled
  We praise thee, O our child."

So with an hundred cities' mouths in one
  Praising thy supreme son,
Son of thy sorrow, O mother, O maid and
    mother,
  Our queen, who serve none other,

E

Our lady of pity and mercy, and full of grace,
    Turn otherwhere thy face,
Turn for a little and look what things are
    these
    Now fallen before thy knees ;
Turn upon them thine eyes who hated thee,
    Behold what things they be,
Italia : these are stubble that were steel,
    Dust, or a turning wheel ;
As leaves, as snow, as sand, that were so
    strong;
    And howl, for all their song,
And wail, for all their wisdom ; they that were
    So great, they are all stript bare,
They are all made empty of beauty, and all
    abhorred ;
    They are shivered, and their sword ;

They are slain who slew, they are heartless
 who were wise;
 Yea, turn on these thine eyes,
O thou, soliciting with soul sublime
 The obscure soul of time,
Thou, with the wounds thy holy body
 bears
 From broken swords of theirs,
Thou, with the sweet swoln eyelids that have
 bled
 Tears for thy thousands dead,
And upon these, whose swords drank up like
 dew
 The sons of thine they slew,
These, whose each gun blasted with murdering
 mouth
 Live flowers of thy fair south,

These, whose least evil told in alien ears
  Turned men's whole blood to tears,
These, whose least sin remembered for pure
    shame
  Turned all those tears to flame,
Even upon these, when breaks the extreme blow
  And all the world cries woe,
When heaven reluctant rains long-suffering fire
  On these and their desire,
When his wind shakes them and his waters
    whelm
  Who rent thy robe and realm,
When they that poured thy dear blood forth
    as wine
  Pour forth their own for thine,
On these, on these have mercy : not in hate,
  But full of sacred fate,

Strong from the shrine and splendid from the
god,
Smite, with no second rod.
Because they spared not, do thou rather
spare :
Be not one thing they were.
Let not one tongue of theirs who hate thee
say
That thou wast even as they.
Because their hands were bloody, be thine
white ;
Show light where they shed night :
Because they are foul, be thou the rather
pure ;
Because they are feeble, endure ;
Because they had no pity, have thou pity.

And thou, O supreme city,

O priestless Rome that shalt be, take in
  trust

Their names, their deeds, their dust,

Who held life less than thou wert; be the
  least

To thee indeed a priest,

Priest and burnt-offering and blood-sacrifice
  Given without prayer or price,

A holier immolation than men wist,
  A costlier eucharist,

A sacrament more saving; bend thine head
  Above these many dead

Once, and salute with thine eternal eyes
  Their lowest head that lies.

Speak from thy lips of immemorial speech
  If but one word for each.

Kiss but one kiss on each thy dead son's mouth
  Fallen dumb or north or south.
And laying but once thine hand on brow and
  breast,
  Bless them, through whom thou art blest.
And saying in ears of these thy dead " Well
  done,"
  Shall they not hear " O son" ?
And bowing thy face to theirs made pale for
  thee,
  Shall the shut eyes not see ?
Yea, through the hollow-hearted world of
  death,
  As light, as blood, as breath,
Shall there not flash and flow the fiery
  sense,
  The pulse of prescience ?

Shall not these know as in times overpast

　Thee loftiest to the last?

For times and wars shall change, kingdoms

　　and creeds,

　And dreams of men, and deeds;

Earth shall grow grey with all her golden

　　things,

　Pale peoples and hoar kings;

But though her thrones and towers of nations

　　fall,

　Death has no part in all;

In the air, nor in the imperishable sea,

　Nor heaven, nor truth, nor thee.

Yea, let all sceptre-stricken nations lie,

　But live thou though they die;

Let their flags fade as flowers that storm can mar,

　But thine be like a star;

Let England's, if it float not for men free,

 Fall, and forget the sea ;

Let France's, if it shadow a hateful head,

 Drop as a leaf drops dead ;

Thine let what storm soever smite the rest

 Smite as it seems him best ;

Thine let the wind that can, by sea or land,

 Wrest from thy banner-hand.

Die they in whom dies freedom, die and

  cease,

 Though the world weep for these ;

Live thou and love and lift when these lie

  dead

 The green and white and red.

O our Republic that shalt bind in bands

 The kingdomless far lands

And link the chainless ages ; thou that wast
  With England ere she past
Among the faded nations, and shalt be
  Again, when sea to sea
Calls through the wind and light of morning
    time,
  And throneless clime to clime
Makes antiphonal answer ; thou that art
  Where one man's perfect heart
Burns, one man's brow is brightened for thy
    sake,
  Thine, strong to make or break ;
O fair Republic hallowing with stretched hands
  The limitless free lands,
When all men's heads for love, not fear, bow
    down
  To thy sole royal crown,

As thou to freedom ; when man's life smells
    sweet,
  And at thy bright swift feet
A bloodless and a bondless world is laid ;
  Then, when thy men are made,
Let these indeed as we in dreams behold
  One chosen of all thy fold,
One of all fair things fairest, one exalt
  Above all fear or fault,
One unforgetful of unhappier men
  And us who loved her then ;
With eyes that outlook suns and dream on
    graves ;
  With voice like quiring waves ;
With heart the holier for their memories'
    sake
  Who slept that she might wake ;

With breast the sweeter for that sweet blood
    lost,
  And all the milkless cost ;
Lady of earth, whose large equality
  Bends but to her and thee ;
Equal with heaven, and infinite of years,
  And splendid from quenched tears ;
Strong with old strength of great things fallen
    and fled,
  Diviner for her dead ;
Chaste of all stains and perfect from all scars,
  Above all storms and stars,
All winds that blow through time, all waves
    that foam,
  Our Capitolian Rome.

THE END.

POEMS AND BALLADS.

By ALGERNON C. SWINBURNE.

Fcap. 8vo, pp. 350, cloth, 9s.

JOHN CAMDEN HOTTEN.

———

Selections from the VERY NUMEROUS
OPINIONS OF THE PRESS
(*English and American*).

" Wherever there is any kind of true genius, we have no right to drive it mad by ridicule or invective; we must deal with it wisely, justly, fairly. Some of the passages which have been selected as evidence of (the poet's) plain speaking, have been wantonly misunderstood. The volume, as a whole, is neither profane nor indecent. A little more clothing in our *uncertain climate* might perhaps have been attended with advantage. . . . . To us this volume, for the first time, conclusively settles that Mr. Swinburne is not a mere brilliant rhetorician or melodious twanger of another man's lyre, but authentically a poet."—FRASER'S MAGAZINE, Nov. 1866.

" There is enough in the volume to have made the fortune of most members of his craft."—THE SCOTSMAN.

" The outcry that has been made over his last published volume of ' Poems and Ballads' is not very creditable to his critics. . . . Old Testament Poetry has fastened upon his imagination quite as strongly as the sublime fatalism of the old Greek dramatists. . . . There is a terrible earnestness about these books. . . . That a book thus dealing with the desire of the flesh should have been denounced as profligate because it does not paint the outside of the Sodom's apple of like colour of the ashes that it shows within, says little indeed for the thoroughness of current criticism."—EXAMINER.

" Coarse animalism, draped with the most seductive hues of art and romance. We will not analyze the poems; we will not even pretend to give the reasons upon which our opinion is based." *For sale by Newcomb & Co., Broadway.*—ALBANY JOURNAL.

" The critics seem to be agreed in seizing upon what deserves reprobation without noticing what deserves respect. In this way he has been either very blindly or very unfairly dealt with."—PALL MALL GAZETTE.

" The theatre of Mr. Swinburne is co-extensive with this knowledge and experience. It will expand, and there is no fear of his being denied an audience, or crushed by a critique. He is more likely to realize the boast of Nelson, who, finding himself unmentioned in the 'Gazette,' declared a day would come when he should have one for himself. We are not in the secret of his own defence, or his reappearance. He may or may not withdraw poems which have been impregnated by designing criticism with a pruriency which was not their own."—READER.

"In every page of these poems we meet with evidences of the fire, the fulness, and the licence of youth. Swinburne is a genuine bard: he sneers at proprieties, he never splits hairs; but gives full vent to his love and hate—his contempt and scorn. He laughs at what other people revere. He would dance in a cathedral."—STIRLING JOURNAL.

" It will be a sad day for English poetry when such volumes as this get read and praised by the better critics, yet the merit of some of the pieces—though by no means high—is greater than of anything heretofore published by this admiring friend of Mr. Jones, Mr. Whistler, and poor old Landor." *For sale by Nichols & Noyes.*—BOSTON COMMONWEALTH.

" This is a collection of miscellaneous pieces of poetry, &c., by that young and promising writer, Mr. Algernon Charles Swinburne. The work, originally brought out by Moxon & Co., has been reprinted by Carleton of this city in a very superior and tasteful style. Of the poems themselves, they are written in all the ardency of youth, but many of the pieces breathe forth a love of freedom, truth and justice in strong but truly poetic language."—NEW YORK WATCHMAN.

" This is a famous book. The critics are not by any means unanimous in their estimate of Swinburne. Some laud him for 'outspoken honesty, earnestness, poetic insight, truth and beauty of expression,' while others regard his poems as even of doubtful morality. That he is a true poet, a master of nervous English, and very bold, no one ought to deny. Whether his poetry is likely to do harm is another question. The ballad commencing

> " If love were what the rose is,
> And I were like the leaf,"

which has lately gone the rounds of the papers, is in this volume, and many others of extraordinary merit as compositions."—RICHMOND DISPATCH, VA.

"Swinburne is undoubtedly a true poet, having a fine power of expression, which is felicitous and ever appropriate. His muse is fired with the stirring fantasies of youth, and his warm desires are told in language which by beauty of expression veils somewhat their grossness."—PHILADELPHIA DISPATCH.

"No writer of modern times has excited so much interest as Algernon Charles Swinburne. Although a very young man, he has exhibited a maturity of intellect that has almost entirely disarmed the critics. The striking originality of his productions has astonished the literary world, and placed him unquestionably in the front rank of English poets. A recent edition of his poems, entitled ' Laus Veneris, and other Poems and Ballads,' however, has subjected him to a more severe ordeal than he has yet met with, and has called forth from his own pen a defence which will be published in the second edition of his new volume.

"There is a music of strength in these poems, outspoken honesty, a sturdy love of freedom, earnestness, poetic insight, truth and beauty of expression, beyond anything attained to by other of the young poets of the day. In some of the poems are the passions of youth fearlessly expressed, and stirring depths that have been stirred hitherto by no poet in his youth."—PHILADELPHIA AGE.

"As our modern critics are very sensitive, the volume of poems was rather warmly denounced. The Moxons were alarmed, and copies were called in as fast as possible. Fortunately one fell in our way, and we read it through, with the light which the virtuous reviewers had flashed upon the book. We found scarcely a poem deserving the censures of the hyper-prudish press. Much was in the manly style in which Landor would write about old Greek stories, much in the bold and nervous style in which any but an emasculated laureate would write about some of the middle age legends and romances. The poems seemed to be bold, manly, vigorous—with none of the effeminacies of Moore, the profanities of Shelley, or the suggestive pruriencies of many modern novelists. We could not help exclaiming, 'Where's the harm?' 'Why decry such poems?' They may have the faults of fulness, the errors of youth, the warmth of passion, but are in no way worse than scores of the poems of half a century ago, and not half so bad as many of the novels of to-day. However, the censors prevailed, and the volume was withdrawn—only to be republished by Mr. J. Camden Hotten, who, as he —unlike Messrs. Moxon—does not sell Shelley's Works, has undertaken to give the present volume to the world."—BIRMINGHAM JOURNAL.

"All his poems are remarkable for their rhythmic beauty and wondrous wealth of language and exquisite imagery. Even when he has but little to say, his manner of saying that little is so musical, that the melody charms us and lingers in the memory like some sweet strain of music."—NEW HAVEN PALLADIUM.

"Any father who finds it in his household, should at once consign it to the flames. *For sale by Newcomb & Co., Broadway.*"—ALBANY JOURNAL.

"It is difficult to imagine what could have been the impelling motive of Mr. Swinburne in offering this collection of his writings to the public. He ought to have been aware that it could in no way enhance his reputation as a writer worthy of his age and time. But indeed it may very safely be said that if he had stopped short after the publication of the ' Atalanta in Calydon,' he would have stood much higher as a poet than he now does. Everything which he has since given us,

'Chastelard,' 'Rosamond,' and now the volume before us, has been a step down-ward. This, it is true, is a literary history not sufficiently uncommon to excite our surprise, but it is none the less a matter of regret. Unfortunately he possesses an extraordinary grace and power of expression, and a melodious felicity in the use of language and of poetic imagery, which sometimes invests his worst verses with a charm that half veils their vileness." *For sale by Davis and Brothers.*—PORTLAND PRESS.

"Let us hope that the kingdom on earth which the poets help advance, and which already owns the constant service of such men as Tennyson, Longfellow, Bryant, Lowell, may not miss the brilliant and subtle power of Swinburne's verse." —BROOKLYN UNION.

"Probably no poet has brought to the simply sensuous delights of love, to the subtle relation by which passion is kindled in heart of man and woman, by which the soul is subdued and disgraced and overwhelmed in intervals of fierce, untam-able joy, to its unutterable anguish following, more of the graces and allurements and bold, unconcealed delineation of passion, than Mr. Swinburne. Byron is coarse and cold beside him. Tom Moore is a wayward, superficial chatterer com-pared to Swinburne. . . . . We have no sympathy with the criticism which denounces Mr. Swinburne and his poetry as hopelessly bad."—BROOKLYN UNION.

"It is time that such works should cease to be palmed off on the public under the names of authors of good repute, and with the imprint of respectable pub-lishers on their title-pages." "In our review of 'Chastelard' we formed so low an estimate of his ability as to deem him an utterly over-estimated young man."—WASHINGTON TELEGRAPH.

"The poems are all strongly characteristic, musical, and gracefully versified. The fatal fault in the eyes of the English critics is the sensual tone of some of the poems, which they exaggerate beyond reason and common sense."—HARTFORD COURANT.

"The book seems to be written, like Charles Reade's 'Griffith Gaunt' and Walt Whitman's 'Leaves of Grass,' in a spirit of protest to what Reade terms the 'prurient prudishness' of the age."—WASHINGTON STAR.

(Translation.)

"There is no form of verse which Swinburne does not handle with mastery. Many of his poems are the most lovely melodies in words. The English language can hardly boast greater triumphs than in some of Swinburne's lyrics. We should like to see whether he will overcome the present pouting of criticism and the public: it is to be hoped that he *will* overcome it, and as soon as possible."—BEILAGE ZUR ZUKUNFT, 14 *February,* 1867. (Berlin.)

NOTES ON
"POEMS AND BALLADS."

By ALGERNON C. SWINBURNE.

8vo, 1s.

JOHN CAMDEN HOTTEN.

OPINIONS OF THE PRESS.

" Mr. Swinburne here speaks for himself without personality of any kind, but with much general expression of scorn, which the small critics have fairly brought down on themselves. It is to be regretted that a young poet, from whom much is to be hoped, should be thus forced into explanations that can only humiliate those by whom they were required."—EXAMINER.

" We have no space to dwell any further upon Mr. Swinburne's defects and excellences. They are both very great and remarkable."—PALL MALL GAZETTE.

" He writes ably and eloquently, in prose worthy of the pen which wrote the lines in ' Atalanta' and ' Chastelard '—earnest, graphic, musical. He asserts with singular force that a poet is not bound to write even for reviewers, that he has his own thoughts to utter, his own taste to please, and while he admits the right of the critic to complain, he only demands that the standard of judgment shall be sound and true. He takes his questioned poems, and shows from what point of view they were written, and how they should be looked at—a point of view that of a thorough English poet, trained in the classics, and unable to see why the grand old stories learned at school and colleges should be mere dry and dusty myths."—BIRMINGHAM JOURNAL.

" He pens some doggrel lines, of which we give a verse, addressed to the reviewers who have condemned his blasphemy and obscenity—

> Lie still in kennel, sleek in stable,
>   Good creatures of the stall or sty;
> Shove snouts for crumbs below the table;
>   Lie still, and rise not up to lie.

It is a degradation to dissect such trash as this. Messrs. Moxon and Co. have been blamed for the part they have played in relation to the ' Poems and Ballads,

The *Examiner* falls foul of these gentlemen, and declares that they are only fit to keep 'a milk-walk for the use of babes.' "—SUNDAY GAZETTE.

" We highly approve of the defence made by Mr. Swinburne of the liberty of writers, and willingly indorse his sentiments :—' Literature, to be worthy of men, must be large, liberal, sincere, and cannot be chaste if she be prudish. Purity and prudishness cannot keep house together. Where free speech and fair play are interdicted, foul hints and evil suggestions are hatched into fœtid life.' "—STIRLING ADVERTISER.

" Terrified by the clamour of a literary clique, Mr. Swinburne's publishers have withdrawn their name from the title-page of his book. . . . We cannot blame a tradesman for declining to carry on the sale of certain goods which may not be to the taste of his best customers or supporters. . . . What we find fault with is that the public are not allowed to form an opinion for themselves on the matter. The function of journalism is to sift the wheat, but not to burn what it conceives to be chaff with unquenchable fire."—THE READER.

"In France, as in Germany, such a misrepresentation as even the foremost journals have given of Mr. Swinburne's Poems would have been impossible. With such abundance of imagination, such plethora of language, such substance of passion, as these volumes contain, there is ample food for literary and philosophical criticism, without resorting to the methods that strove to crush Leigh Hunt, Hazlitt, and Shelley and Keats, that found profligacy in ' Rimini ' and blasphemy in 'Adonais.' "—EXAMINER.

"Under the title of 'Notes on Poems and Reviews,' Mr. Algernon Charles Swinburne has just published, with Mr. Hotten, of Piccadilly, what he apparently designs to be a crushing reply to the whole body of his critics, and a triumphant vindication of his own poetic reputation. We, the *Sun*, however, think the task thus undertaken with so much audacity, was in itself too flagrantly outrageous to prove otherwise than an inevitable *fiasco*.' "— THE SUN.

" That his genius is dramatic—finely dramatic—we have taken the liberty to observe on other occasions; it is certain, too, that whatever this dramatic genius writes, is dramatically written ; and it is past all dispute, that what a man writes in that way is not to be taken as 'the assertion of its author's own feeling and faith.' "—PALL MALL GAZETTE.

"Swinburne—like Byron—has replied to his critics, not in a poem, but in a prose pamphlet, entitled ' Notes on Poems and Reviews.' He takes up his poems one by one, tells why he wrote them and what he meant, defends himself from the charge of vulgarity, and cites classical authority without stint. Mr. Swinburne declares he has never written for the purblind or the prurient."—WM. CULLEN BRYANT'S N. Y. EVENING POST.

" Mr. Swinburne's defence of his poems is well timed. Attacks so intemperate as those to which his recent volume of Poems and Ballads was subjected lead almost of necessity to a reaction . . . Gradually this reaction has set in with strong and what might easily become dangerous force. Men whose opinions carry the highest weight in England have pronounced in favour of the victim of so brutal an attack, and the most respected organs of public opinion are attempting the rehabilitation of the clever—if too daring young poet. Like all Mr. Swinburne's prose compositions, it has the advantage of a splendid style . . . a specimen of English prose. We have a high worship of morality, but have no respect whatever for philistinism, and English prudery is the worst and least worthy form of philistinism in existence. Mr. Swinburne's merits are so great that when, indignant at the pitifulness of English society, and the littleness of English art, he kicks over the traces, he should obtain indulgence rather than misrepresentation."—SUNDAY TIMES.

"These [just quoted] passages contain Mr. Swinburne's answer to his detractors. The rest of the pamphlet has in it the scorn that a warm-blooded young poet must feel for that which produced the need of such an explanation."—EXAMINER.

NEW WORK BY MR. SWINBURNE.

ESSAYS ON THE LIFE AND WORKS

OF

WILLIAM BLAKE,

POET AND ARTIST.

Will be shortly published, in 8vo,

WITH ILLUSTRATIONS IN COLOURED FAC SIMILE.

JOHN CAMDEN HOTTEN.

"He is known to have in the press an elaborate study upon the poet and painter Blake—a subject than which none requires more delicate or sharp manipulation, more keenness or speciality of sympathy, or more boldness of estimate and statement. To judge from his own powers in the poetic art, and from his Essay on Byron, Mr. Swinburne will supply all these requisites in a measure hardly to be rivalled."—ROSSETTI'S "CRITICISM."

ROSSETTI'S CRITICISM.

SWINBURNE'S

POEMS AND BALLADS.

A Criticism.

By WILLIAM MICHAEL ROSSETTI.

Fcap. 8vo, cloth, 3s. 6d.

JOHN CAMDEN HOTTEN.

["Let us for a moment stoop to the arbitration of popular breath. Let us assume that Homer was a drunkard, that Virgil was a flatterer, that Horace was a coward, that Tasso was a madman, observe in what a ludicrous chaos the imputations of real or fictitious crime have been confused in the contemporary calumnies against poetry and poets."—SHELLEY.]

" For a criticism friendly by bias, as the author freely admits, as well as by the force of sincere critical admiration, this essay of Mr. Rossetti's on Mr. Swinburne's recent volume is a very candid one, and also one of true critical insight. . . On the whole the criticism of this essay is true criticism and good criticism, however inadequately it estimates some of Mr. Swinburne's greatest faults." — SPECTATOR.

"Subtle criticism, gracefully and temperately expressed. This volume is an exhaustive essay on all Mr. Swinburne's published works."—THE GLOBE.

" An accomplished and gifted critic has undertaken the defence. . . A more difficult thing has seldom been better done. .. He writes about poets and poetry with a subtle apprehensiveness and discrimination which gives to his remarks a real critical value. The poems of Mr. Swinburne are a fact in English literature. As an able and well-weighed effort to assist and hasten the calm judgment of the future, we think Mr. Rossetti's criticism deserves praise. Mr. Swinburne is a remarkable and original poet. . . his position as an artist is beyond dispute or even attack."—SATURDAY REVIEW, 17th November, 1866.

" Mr. Rossetti has had a difficult task to perform, but he has performed it in the very best spirit. The critic writes with great candour and fairness; he has not written in the manner of a partisan. We cordially agree with all the author says, on literary grounds, of the power of Mr. Swinburne's genius."— LONDON REVIEW, 1st December, 1866.

NEW BOOKS NOW READY.

NEW BOOKS NOW READY.

Now ready, 4to. 10s. 6d. on toned paper, very elegant.
Bianca: Poems and Ballads. By Edward Brennan.

Shortly.
The Prometheus Bound of Æschylus Translated in the
Original Metres, by C. B. CAYLEY, B.A.

In a few days, price 2s. 6d.
Never Caught; Personal Adventures during Twelve Successful
Trips in Blockade-Running, 1863-4. By Captain ROBERTS.

Immediately.
Artemus Ward's Popular Books. New Editions under the late
Author's Superintendence.

" It is my wish that with Mr. Hotten alone the right of publishing my books
in England should rest." *Charles F. Browne* (" *Artemus Ward*").

Shortly.
Slang Dictionary. A New Edition.

THE NEW RIDDLE-BOOK.
Now ready, 4to. 7s. 6d. plain ; 8s. 6d. in gold and coloured cover.
Puniana; or, Thoughts Wise and Otherwise. 3,000 Riddles and
10,000 Puns.

THE ENGLISH GUSTAVE DORE.
Now ready, 5s. plain, 7s. 6d. coloured.
Legends of Savage Life. Companion to " The Hatchet Throwers."
Inimitably droll Illustrations, by ERNEST GRISET.

A BOOK TO ENJOY AND LAUGH OVER.
Now ready. 12s.
Seymour's Sketches. The Book of Cockney Sports, Whims, and
Oddities. 180 humorous Drawings, uniform with " Leech's Sketches."

NEW BOOK OF POPULAR HUMOUR.
Now ready, toned paper, 3s. 6d.
Wit and Humour. By the " Autocrat of the Breakfast Table."
A volume of delightfully humorous Poems, similar to Tom Hood.

ANGLICAN CHURCH ORNAMENTS.
This day, thick 8vo. with Illustrations, price 15s.
English Church Furniture, Ornaments, and Decorations, at the
Period of the Reformation, as exhibited in the List of Church Goods destroyed
in certain Lincolnshire Churches, A.D. 1566. Edited by EDWARD PEACOCK,
F.S.A.

. Very curious, as showing what articles of Church Furniture were in those
days considered to be idolatrous or unnecessary. The work, of which only a limited
number has been printed, is of the highest interest to those who take part in the
present Ritual discussion. *See Reviews in the religious Journals.*

Popular and Interesting Books,

PUBLISHED OR SOLD

By JOHN CAMDEN HOTTEN,

74 & 75 PICCADILLY, LONDON, W.

*** NOTE.—*In order to insure the correct delivery of the actual Works, or Particular Editions, specified in this List, the name of the Publisher should be distinctly given. Stamps or a Post Office Order may be remitted direct to the Publisher, who will forward per return.*

Anacreon's Odes. Didot's exquisite Edition, printed in very beautiful Greek characters, with French notes. 12mo. Illustrated with 54 charming Photographs, from compositions by Girodet, in the purest classical style, and of most surpassing beauty and softness. 40s.

The original drawings cost £5,000. The volume is, without exception, the most lovable book ever sent forth by a prodigal publisher. Direct application must be made to Mr. Hotten for this work.

Anecdotes of the Green Room and Stage: or, Leaves from an Actor's Note-Book, at Home and Abroad. By GEORGE VANDENHOFF. Post 8vo, pp. 336, price 2s.

Includes Original Anecdotes of the Keans (father and son), the two Kembles, Macready, Cooke, Liston, Farren, Elliston, Braham and his Sons, Phelps, Buckstone, Webster, Charles Matthews; Siddons, Vestris, Helen Faucit, Mrs. Nisbet, Miss Cushman, Miss O'Neil, Mrs. Glover, Mrs. Charles Kean, Rachel, Ristori, and many other dramatic celebrities.

AN INTERESTING VOLUME TO ANTIQUARIES.

Now ready, 4to. half-morocco, handsomely printed, price 7s. 6d.

Army Lists of the Roundheads and Cavaliers in the Civil War.

These most curious Lists show on which side the gentlemen of England were to be found during the great conflict between the King and the Parliament. Only a very few copies have been most carefully reprinted on paper that will gladden the heart of the lover of choice books.

This day, Sixth Thousand, price 1s.; by post 1s. 2d.

Artemus Ward—His Book. Edited, with Notes and Introduction, by the Editor of the 'Biglow Papers.' One of the wittiest and certainly the most mirth-provoking book which has been published for many years.

'He is as clever as Thackeray in Jeames's Dialogue and Policeman X's ballads ... There is no merriment in him; it is all dry, sparkling humour.'—SPECTATOR.

This day, 4th edition, on tinted paper, bound in cloth, neat, price 3s. 6d.; by post 3s. 10d.

Artemus Ward. The 'Author's Edition;' containing, in addition to the above, two extra chapters, entitled, 'The Draft in Baldinsville,' with Mr. Ward's Private Opinion concerning Old Bachelors,' and 'Mr. W.'s Visit to a Graffick' [Soiree].

'We never, not even in the pages of our best humorists, read anything so laughable and so shrewd as we have seen in this book by the mirthful Artemus.'—PUBLIC OPINION.

Baron Munchausen, Adventures de. Illustrated with 220

Fantastic and Extraordinary Wood Engravings by GUSTAVE DORÉ. 4to. cloth elegant, 19s. 6d. With a portrait of the renowned Baron, and his motto, ' Mendace Veritas.'

Nothing can exceed the drollery and humour of these wonderful and inimitable Illustrations. Direct application must be made to Mr. Hotten for this work.

Berjeau's (P. C.) Book of Dogs; the Varieties of Dogs as

they are found in Old Sculptures, Pictures, Engravings, and Books. 1865. Half-morocco, the sides richly lettered with gold, 7s. 6d.

In this very interesting volume are 52 plates, facsimiled from rare old Engravings, Paintings, Sculptures, &c., in which may be traced over 100 varieties of Dogs known to the Ancients.

12th Thousand, beautifully printed, 12mo. neat, 1s.; by post, 1s. 2d.

THE CHOICEST HUMOROUS POETRY OF THE AGE. THE

Biglow Papers. By James Russell Lowell.

*** This Edition has been edited, with additional Notes explanatory of the persons and subjects mentioned therein, and is the only complete and correct Edition published in this country. ' The celebrated " Biglow Papers." '—TIMES, July 25th.

Book of Common Prayer. Pickering's sumptuous Folio

Edition, Printed Red and Black, in Bold Old English Letter, on the finest vellum paper—a truly regal volume. Half-vellum, very neat (sells £7 7s.), only 38s., or bound in half-morocco in the Roxburghe style, £2 7s. 6d.

☞ Admirably adapted for use in the pulpit or reading stand. With lovers of choice books is not unfrequently termed the ' Cathedral Edition.'

Apply direct for this work.

Common Prayer. Illustrated by Holbein and Albert

Dürer. With wood-engravings of the ' Life of Christ,' rich woodcut border on every page of Fruit and Flowers; also the Dance of Death, a singularly curious series after Holbein, with Scriptural Quotations and Proverbs in the Margin. Square 8vo. cloth neat, exquisitely printed on tinted paper, price 10s. 6d.; in dark morocco, very plain and neat, with block in the Elizabethian style impressed on the sides, gilt edges, 17s. 6d.

Apply direct for this exquisite volume.

AN EXTRAORDINARY BOOK.

Beautifully printed, thick 8vo. new half-morocco, gilt-back, 14s. 6d.

Contes Drolatiques (Droll Tales collected from the Abbeys

of Loraine). Par BALZAC. With Four Hundred and Twenty-five Marvellous, Extravagant, and Fantastic Woodcuts, by GUSTAVE DORÉ.

The most singular designs ever attempted by any artist. This book is a fund of amusement So crammed is it with pictures that even the contents are adorned with thirty-three Illustrations Direct application must be made to Mr. Hotten for this work.

Now ready, price 2s. 6d.; by post 2s. 10d.

Dictionary of the Oldest Words in the English Language,

from the Semi-Saxon Period of A.D. 1250 to 1300; consisting of an Alphabetical Inventory of Every Word found in the printed English Literature of the 13th Century, by the late HERBERT COLERIDGE, Secretary to the Philological Society. 8vo. neat half-morocco.

An invaluable work to historical students and those interested in linguistic pursuits.

Forster and Foster Family. Some Account of the

Forsters of Cold Hesledon, in the County Palatine of Durham. Also the Fosters of other parts of England. By J. FOSTER. 4to. exquisitely printed on tinted paper, with Emblazoned Coat Armour of the Family of Forster, or Foster. 12s. 6d. Sunderland, printed 1862.

HERALDRY OF WALES.

Only 50 copies printed, in marvellous facsimile, 4to. on old Welsh paper, half-morocco, 12s. 6d.

Display of Herauldry of the particular Coat Armours now

in use in the Six Counties in North Wales, and several others elsewhere; with the Names of the Families, whereby any man knowing from what family he is descended, may know his particular Arms. By JOHN REYNOLDS, of Oswestry, Antiquarian; with nearly One Hundred Coat Armours Blazoned in the Old Style. Chester, printed 1739.

From a Unique Copy, of priceless value to the lover of Heraldry and Genealogy.

AN ENTIRELY NEW BOOK OF DELIGHTFUL FAIRY TALES.

Now ready, square 12mo. handsomely printed on toned paper, in cloth, green and gold, price 4s. 6d. plain, 5s. 6d. coloured (by post, 6d. extra).

Family Fairy Tales; or, Glimpses of Elfland at Heatherston

Hall. Edited by CHOLMONDELEY PENNELL, Author of 'Puck on Pegasus,' &c., adorned with beautiful pictures of 'My Lord Lion,' 'King Uggermugger,' and other great folks.

This charming volume of Original Tales has been universally praised by the critical press.

Now ready, in 8vo. on tinted paper, nearly 350 pages, very neat, price 5s.

Family History of the English Counties: Descriptive

Account of Twenty Thousand most Curious and Rare Books, Old Tracts, Ancient Manuscripts, Engravings, and Privately Printed Family Papers, relating to the History of almost every Landed Estate and Old English Family in the Country; interspersed with nearly Two Thousand Original Anecdotes, Topographical and Antiquarian Notes. By JOHN CAMDEN HOTTEN.

By far the largest collection of English and Welsh Topography and Family History ever formed. Each article has a small price affixed for the convenience of those who may desire to possess any book or tract that interests them.

Gustave Doré. La Légende de Croque-Mitaine Recueillie,

par ERNEST L'EPINE. 4to. Illustrated with nearly 200 Marvellous, Extravagant, and Fantastic Woodcuts. By GUSTAVE DORÉ. 19s. 6d.

In this mad volume Doré has surpassed all his former efforts. The illustrations are, without exception, the most wonderful ever put into a book. Direct application must be made to Mr. Hotten for this book

---

Now ready, handsomely printed, price 1s. 6d.

Hints on Hats, adapted to the Heads of the People. By

HENRY MELTON, of Regent Street. With curious Woodcuts of the various styles of Hats worn at different periods.

Anecdotes of eminent and fashionable personages are given, and a fund of interesting information relative to the History of Costume and change of tastes may be found scattered through its pages.

This day, handsomely bound, pp. 550, price 7s. 6d.

History of Playing Cards, with Anecdotes of their Use

in Ancient and Modern Games, Conjuring, Fortune-Telling, and Card-Sharping. With Sixty curious Illustrations on toned paper.

Skill and Sleight of Hand.	Card Revels and Blind Hookey.
Gambling and Calculation.	Piquet and Vingt-et-un.
Cartomancy and Cheating.	Whist and Cribbage.
Old Games and Gaming-Houses.	Old-Fashioned Tricks.

' A highly-interesting volume.'—MORNING POST.

Horatii Opera. Didot's Exquisite Edition, in small but

very legible type, with numerous most beautiful Photographs from Paintings. 30s. Bound in the finest polished morocco, exquisitely finished and gilt, ; or with elaborately-tooled sides, after an ancient pattern, 55s.

Direct application must be made to Mr. Hotten for this work.

EVERY HOUSEKEEPER SHOULD POSSESS A COPY.

Now ready, in cloth, price 2s. 6d. ; by post 2s. 8d.   The

Housekeeper's Assistant ; a Collection of the most valuable

Recipes, carefully written down for future use, by Mrs. B——, during her forty years' active service.

☞ As much as two guineas has been paid for a copy of this invaluable little work.

THE ORIGINAL EDITION OF JOE MILLER'S JESTS. 1739.

Joe Miller's Jests ; or, the Wit's Vade Mecum ; a Collec-

tion of the most Brilliant Jests, politest Repartees, most elegant Bons Mots, and most pleasant short Stories in the English Language.   An interesting specimen of remarkable facsimile, 8vo. half-morocco, price 9s. 6d.   London : printed by T. Read, 1739.

Only a very few copies of this humorous book have been reproduced.

Now ready, 12mo. very choicely printed, price 6s. 6d.

London Directory for 1677.   The Earliest Known List of

the London Merchants.   See Review in the *Times*, Jan. 22.

This curious little volume has been reprinted verbatim from one of the only two copies known to be in existence.   It contains an Introduction pointing out some of the principal persons mentioned in the list.   For historical and genealogical purposes the little book is of the greatest value.   Herein will be found the originators of many of the great firms and co-partnerships which have prospered through two pregnant centuries, and which exist some of them in nearly the same names at this day.   Its most distinctive feature is the early severance which it marks of 'goldsmiths that keep running cashes,' precursors of the modern bankers, from the mass of the merchants of London.

Now ready, price 5s. ; by post, on roller, 5s. 4d.

Magna Charta.   An Exact Facsimile of the Original

Document, preserved in the British Museum, very carefully drawn, and printed on fine plate paper, nearly 3 feet long by 2 wide, with the Arms and Seals of the Barons elaborately emblazoned in gold and colours.   A.D. 1215.

Copied by express permission, and the only correct drawing of the Great Charter ever taken. Handsomely framed and glazed, in carved oak, of an antique pattern, 22s. 6d.   It is uniform with the 'Roll of Battle Abbey.'
A full translation, with Notes, has just been prepared, price 6d.

This day, neatly printed, price 1s. 6d. ; by post 1s. 8d.

Mental Exertion: Its Influence on Health.   By Dr.

BRIGHAM.   Edited, with additional Notes, by Dr. ARTHUR LEARED, Physician to the Great Northern Hospital.   This is a highly important little book, showing how far we may educate the mind without injuring the body.

The recent untimely deaths of Admiral Fitzroy and Mr. Prescott, whose minds gave way under excessive mental exertion, fully illustrate the importance of the subject.

Millais Family, the Lineage and Pedigree of, recording

its History from 1331 to 1865, by J. BERTRAND PAYNE, with Illustrations from Designs by the Author.   Folio, exquisitely printed on toned paper, with numerous Etchings, &c., price 28s.

Of this beautiful volume only sixty copies have been privately printed for presents to the several members of the family.   The work is magnificently bound in blue and gold.   These are believed to be the only etchings of an Heraldic character ever designed and engraved by the distinguished artist of the name.

Apply direct for this work.

GUNTER'S CONFECTIONERY.

Now ready, 8vo. with numerous Illustrations, price 6s. 6d.   The

Modern Confectioner: a Practical Guide to the most

improved methods for making the various kinds of Confectionery ; with the manner of preparing and laying out Desserts ; adapted for private families or large establishments.   By WILLIAM JEANES, Chief Confectioner at Messrs. Gunter's (Confectioners to Her Majesty), Berkeley Square.

All housekeepers should have it.'   DAILY TELEGRAPH.

ANECDOTES OF THE 'LONG PARLIAMENT' OF 1645.

Now ready, in 4to. half-morocco, choicely printed, price 7s. 6d. The

Mystery of the Good Old Cause: Sarcastic Notices of those

Members of the Long Parliament that held places, both Civil and Military, contrary to the self-denying Ordinance of April 3, 1645; with the sums of money and lands they divided among themselves.

Gives many curious particulars about the famous Assembly not mentioned by historians or biographers The history of almost every county in England receives some illustration from it Genealogists and antiquaries will find in it much interesting matter.

Pansie; a Child Story, the Last Literary Effort of Nathaniel Hawthorne. 12mo. price 6d.

This day, in 2 vols. 8vo. very handsomely printed, price 16s.

THE HOUSEHOLD STORIES OF ENGLAND.

Popular Romances of the West of England; or, the

Drolls of Old Cornwall. Collected and edited by ROBERT HUNT, F.R.S.

For an analysis of this important work see printed description, which may be obtained gratis at the Publisher's.

Many of the Stories are remarkable for their wild poetic beauty; others surprise us by their quaintness; whilst others, again, show forth a tragic force which can only be associated with those rude ages which existed long before the period of authentic history.

Mr. George Cruikshank has supplied two wonderful pictures as illustrations to the work. One is a portrait of Giant Bolster, a personage 12 miles high.

The hitherto Unknown Poem, written by John Bunyan, whilst confined in Bedford Jail, for the support of his Family, entitled

Profitable Meditations, Fitted to Man's Different Condition: in a Conference between Christ and a Sinner. By JOHN BUNYAN, Servant to the Lord Jesus Christ. Small 4to. half-morocco, very neat, price 7s. 6d. The few remaining copies now offered at 4s. 6d.

'A highly interesting memorial of the great allegorist.'—ATHENÆUM.

THE NEW BOOK OF HUMOROUS VERSE.

Now ready, in sq. 8vo. full gilt (price 7s. 6d.); a few copies at 3s. 6d. each.

Puck on Pegasus. By H. Cholmondeley Pennell. With

numerous Illustrations, by JOHN LEECH, GEORGE CRUIKSHANK, TENNIEL, 'PHIZ' (HABLOT K. BROWNE), and JULIAN PORTCH.

Robson; a Sketch, by George Augustus Sala. An interesting Biography, with sketches of his famous characters, 'Jem Baggs,' 'Boots at the Swan,' 'The Yellow Dwarf,' 'Daddy Hardacre,' &c. Price 6d.

Uniform with 'Magna Charta.'

Roll of Battle Abbey; or, a List of the Principal Warriors

who came over from Normandy with William the Conqueror and settled in this country. A.D. 1066-7, from Authentic Documents, very carefully drawn, and printed on fine plate paper, nearly three feet long by two feet wide, with the Arms of the principal Barons elaborately emblazoned in gold and colours, price 5s.; by post, on roller, 5s. 4d.

Handsomely framed and glazed, in carved oak, of an antique pattern, price 22s. 6d.

Now ready, in 4to. very handsomely printed, with curious woodcut initial letters extra cloth, 18s.; or crimson morocco extra, the sides and back covered in rich fleur-de-lys, gold tooling, 55s.

Roll of Carlaverlock; with the Arms of the Earls, Barons,

and Knights who were present at the Siege of this Castle in Scotland, 28 Edward I., A.D. 1300; including the Original Anglo-Norman Poem, and an English Translation of the MS. in the British Museum; the whole newly edited by THOMAS WRIGHT, Esq., M.A., F.S.A.

A very handsome volume, and a delightful one o lovers of Heraldry, as it is the earliest blazon or arms known to exist.

Shakspeare's Dramatic Works. One of a few Copies on a

fine and beautiful paper, the illustrations by Stothard, with charming little ornamental head-pieces, half-morocco, very neat, top edge crimsoned, contents lettered, 10 vols. post 8vo. (sells at £6 15s. unbound) 58s. only ; or in yellow (or green), calf extra and delicately-tooled backs, £5 18s. Whittingham, 1856.
Direct application must be made to Mr. Hotten for this work.

Slang Dictionary; or, The Vulgar Words, Street Phrases,

and ' Fast' Expressions of High and Low Society ; many with their Etymology, and a few with their History traced. With curious illustrations. Pp. 328, in 8vo. price 6s. 6d.; by post 7s.

One hundred and forty newspapers in this country alone have reviewed with approbation this Dictionary of Colloquial English. The Times devoted three columns to explain its merits, and the little John o' Groat's Journal gave its modest paragraph in eulogy. ' It may be doubted of there exists a more amusing volume in the English language.'—Spectator. ' Valuable as a work of reference.'—Saturday Review. ' All classes of society will find amusement and instruction in its pages.'—Times.

Thackeray: The Humourist and the Man of Letters. The

Story of his Life and Literary Labours. With some particulars of his Early Career never before made public. By THEODORE TAYLOR, Esq., Membre de la Société des Gens de Lettres. Price 7s. 6d.

Illustrated with Photographic Portrait (one of the most characteristic known to have been taken) by Ernest Edwards, B.A.; view of Mr. Thackeray's House, built after a favourite design of the great Novelist's; facsimile of his Handwriting, long noted in London literary circles for its exquisite neatness; and a curious little sketch of his Coat of Arms, a pen and pencil humorously introduced as the crest, the motto, ' Nobilitas est sola virtus' (Virtue is the sole nobility).

Now ready, with nearly 300 Drawings from Nature.

The Young Botanist: a Popular Guide to Elementary

Botany. By T. S. RALPH, of the Linnæan Society. Price 2s. 6d. plain: 4s. coloured by hand.

An excellent book for the young beginner. The objects selected as illustrations are either easy of access as specimens of wild plants, or are common in gardens.

Virgilii Opera, ed. Joannis Bond. Didot's exquisite edition,

in small but very legible type, with numerous most beautiful Photographs, from Paintings by M. BARRIAS. 24mo. 35s. The most exquisite Classically illustrated edition of Virgil ever published. Choicely bound in morocco of the finest quality, tooled and gilt in the most finished style, 58s.; or with elaborately tooled sides, after an ancient pattern, £3 5s.
Direct application must be made to Mr. Hotten for this work.

BEST FRENCH LESSON BOOK EVER PUBLISHED
Ordinary price, 5s. ; a few copies now offered at 3s. 6d.

Vocabulaire Symbolique. A Symbolic French and Eng-

lish Vocabulary for Students of every age. By RAGONET. Illustrated by many hundred Woodcuts, exhibiting familiar objects of every description, with French and English explanations, thus stamping the French terms and phrases indelibly on the mind.
Direct application must be made to Mr. Hotten for this work.

Warrant to Execute Charles I. An Exact Facsimile of

this Important Document in the House of Lords, with the Fifty-nine Signatures of the Regicides, and Corresponding Seals, admirably executed on paper made to imitate the original Document, 22 in. by 14 in. Price 2s.; by post, 2s. 4d.
Handsomely framed and glazed, in carved oak, of an antique pattern, 14s. 6d.

NOW READY.

Warrant to Execute Mary Queen of Scots. The Exact

Facsimile of this Important Document, including the Signature of Queen Elizabeth and Facsimile of the Great Seal, on tinted paper, made to imitate the original MS. Safe on roller, 2s.; by post, 2s. 4d.
Handsomely framed and glazed, in carved oak, of an antique pattern 4s. 6d.